Totally

bindi

ACCESS ALL AREAS

Totally bindi

ACCESS ALL AREAS

RANDOM HOUSE AUSTRALIA

A Random House book
Published by Random House Australia Pty Ltd
Level 3, 100 Pacific Highway, North Sydney NSW 2060
www.randomhouse.com.au

First published by Random House Australia in 2010

Addresses for companies within the Random House Group can be found at www.randomhouse.com.au/offices

National Library of Australia
Cataloguing-in-Publication entry

Author: Black, Jess
Title: Totally Bindi! / Jess Black and Bindi Irwin
ISBN: 978 1 86471 858 4 (pbk.)
Target Audience: For children
Subjects: Irwin, Bindi, 1998–
Other Authors/Contributors: Irwin, Bindi, 1998–
Dewey Number: 333.72092

Front cover photograph © Getty Images
Back cover photographs © Australia Zoo
Cover, internal design and typesetting by Liz Seymour, Seymour Designs
All internal illustrations © Australia Zoo, except for the images on pp. 23, 40, 73 and 83 © Getty Images

Printed in China by Midas Printing International Limited

10 9 8 7 6 5 4 3 2 1

Mixed Sources
Product group from well-managed
forests and other controlled sources
www.fsc.org Cert no. SGS-COC-003843
© 1996 Forest Stewardship Council
FSC

Contents

Get Up Close and Personal* with Bindi!

Everything you ever wanted to know about Bindi (and more)

Full name Bindi Sue Irwin

Age 12

Birthday 24 July 1998

Bindi in five words Determined, caring, passionate, Wildlife Warrior

Star sign Leo

Nickname Beetle

Pets A German Shepherd called Diamond and a horse named Harry.

Fave TV show *Friends* because it makes me laugh.

Fave food Mango, it's a healthy snack and reminds me of summer.

Fave book I love *Black Beauty* because it's about horses and I love them. I really enjoy reading because I'm in a different world when I read.

Fave movie *Grease*, because it's got lots of great songs and because John Travolta and Olivia Newton-John are in it.

Fave colour Pink because it makes me feel happy and it brightens up the whole day.

Fave song to perform 'Macaw', 'My Dad', and all the other *Bindi: The Jungle Girl* songs. I like them because they're fun, energetic and because they're my songs and lots of other kids can relate to them.

Fave thing to do I love playing at Australia Zoo because there's so much to do and see. I also think hanging out with my best friend Rosie is great fun. You can never have enough time with friends!

Fave article of clothing I love all the tops and jeans in the Bindi Wear International line because I can play in them and get dirty in them and it will all come out. I can also climb trees in them!

Fave accessory I am a sucker for a nice handbag. Every once in a while I like being a girly girl.

Fave saying/motto 'Treat animals how you would like to be treated' and 'The only place where success comes before work is in the dictionary'.

Fave musician The Veronicas are my favourites because they are lovely girls with great music as well as being Ambassadors for Wildlife Warriors.

Bindi's Bestie

Bindi thinks best friends are just the best thing ever!

Bindi's best friend's name is Rosie Harris. She has known her since she was four years old. They met in preschool and have been best friends ever since. Rosie has two brothers and one sister and she lives in Ipswich. Rosie has a dog named Daisy and she loves animals and especially horses, just like Bindi. They have been on a lot of adventures together including going to Lady Elliot Island, taking surf lessons and horse riding lessons. Rosie was also the first person to have a sleepover with Bindi.

We asked Bindi all about friendship and what it means to her

What qualities do you look for in a friend?
They have to be kind, funny, interesting and trustworthy.

Why is friendship important to you?
Friendship is so important to me because a friend is someone you can count on, someone you can tell all your secrets to and they will be there for you through the ups and downs.

Do you think you are a good friend to others, and why?
Yes, I am a good friend because no matter what is happening in my friend's life they know they can count on me to be there for them. Even if it's just a smile to say everything is going to be okay or a hug to say well done. We also have an occasional scream of excitement together.

Do you have any animal friends?
I have a lot of animal friends because I am so lucky to live in a zoo, but I also have Diamond, my German Shepherd dog and my horse, Harry. I love taking Diamond to the beach and swimming in the waves with her and riding Harry is great because I feel like I'm free.

What are some of your favourite things to do with your best friend?
We love to play around the zoo and visit all the animals. We also love to play tag and stuck in the mud together – we really never get bored of them. Sometimes we build massive box cubbies and cook our own lunch. Spaghetti bolognaise and cupcakes are our favourites.

Animal Magnetism Quiz

Have a go at this fun quiz to work out what kind of animal you are, based on your personality!

Every animal has its own different traits and qualities that make it unique. What kind of animal do you think you are closest to in behaviour, likes and dislikes?

Are you a fierce tiger or a wiry wolf? Do you like to make a splash like a dolphin or are you more of a Bambi in personality? Perhaps you see yourself as a great big bear!

You'll not only have heaps of fun giving your answers but you'll also learn a few new things about yourself and animals!

1. What is your favourite kind of party?
a. A slumber party
b. A surprise party
c. A fancy dress party
d. A pool party
e. You don't like parties

2. What makes you upset?
a. Being woken up
b. Someone invading your territory
c. Being rushed or jostled
d. People who litter
e. Anyone threatening your family

3. When you are at a party, you like to . . .
a. Give great presents
b. Win at party games
c. Be the centre of attention
d. Make new friends
e. Hang out on your own, you are very shy

4. What is your favourite colour?
a. Brown
b. Orange
c. Gold
d. Blue
e. Grey

5. What is your favourite meal?
a. Blueberry and honey pancakes
b. A big, juicy steak
c. A healthy salad
d. Sushi
e. A chicken dinner

6. Your favourite holiday would involve . . .

a. Staying at home and watching TV
b. Hiking in the woods
c. A luxurious five star hotel and shopping
d. Surfing at the beach
e. Being with your family

7. Your dream job is . . .

a. Builder
b. Explorer
c. Ballet dancer
d. Marine biologist
e. Entrepreneur

8. What's your favourite pastime?

a. Fishing
b. Swimming
c. Shopping
d. Diving
e. Running

9. What time of the day do you have the most energy?

a. First thing in the morning
b. Later in the day
c. During the daylight hours
d. Early evening
e. At night

10. If you could have a super power, what would it be?

a. Super strength
b. Night vision
c. Super senses
d. Swim like Aquaman
e. Run like the wind

How did you score?

Circle the letters scored alongside your answers and count up the letter that appears most often. This is your most dominant animal personality!

Mostly As BEAR

You are down-to-earth and practical. Bear is the voice of reason. Bear is gifted with an enormous heart, and is very generous. You can be modest and shy. You have great patience and can be reclusive and a little on the lazy side!

Mostly Bs TIGER

You are patient but short-tempered, calm but rebellious, petty but noble, fearsome but affectionate, a free spirit but fiercely territorial. You have lots of difficulty making up your mind about things! Tiger shows natural leadership ability, but prefers to work alone.

Mostly Cs DEER

You are beautiful! Deer is quick-witted with a great sense of humour. You are excellent at communicating and a great conversationalist. You like to always look your best and can be a little self-involved. Deers are so much fun that their friends will tend to overlook any faults. You can be a bit of a drama queen!

Mostly Ds DOLPHIN

You are playful and intelligent. Dolphin is in harmony with the world around it. Friendship is important to you and you are generally very content. Surf that dolphin energy!

Mostly Es WOLF

You are very independent and a bit of a loner at times. You need your freedom but you also need a nurturing environment. Family is very important to you. You are tremendously loyal. Wolf is generous, affectionate and loving.

What's For Lunch?

Feel a snack attack coming on? So do these animals! It's survival of the fittest out in the wild but you'd be surprised by what some animals actually eat, and just how much!

Lions

Lions prey on zebra, antelope, buffalo, oryx and just about any other animal they can find. They might steal food from other predators or feed on a carcass.

White Rhinos

These guys are so big but they are grazers and only eat grass. In the zoo they also like different types of lucerne.

Echidnas

That long snout is excellent for sniffing out ants, termites and other insects in the wild. In the zoo echidnas will also eat worms, minced meat, raw eggs and olive oil.

Pandas

Pandas need bamboo shoots to survive. They prefer to eat the leaves and can gobble as many as 200,000 of them in a single day!

Poison Dart Frogs

These little fellows love insects on their menu - especially maggots, flies and crickets!

Bears

Bears are omnivores yet most of their diet consists of nuts, berries, fruit, leaves and roots. Bears also eat other animals, from rodents to moose, but meat makes up a very small part of their diet. When there are lots of fish, brown and black bears will often fish in the same river as other bears.

Sharks

Sharks eat almost anything – from plankton to large fish, and marine animals – but rarely humans! Sometimes known as the rubbish bins of the sea, tiger sharks have a varied diet that can consist of fish, seals, sharks, livestock that falls into the ocean, even nails, tin cans and shoes!

Harriet the tortoise just loved eating hibiscus flowers!

Under the Spotlight

Five things you didn't know about Bindi!
(SSSHHH, IT'S A SECRET.)

1 She puts her money where her mouth is. Bindi has a heart of gold and regularly raises funds for the Australia Zoo Wildlife Hospital by doing odd jobs for the zoo crew or busking for visitors with impromptu performances. Bindi often gives her own pocket money to the hospital to help all of the sick and injured animals.

2 Bindi LOVES horses. There are pony rides at the zoo and Bindi can hardly tear herself away.

3 One time, when camping in the bush with her family, she woke up in her swag and announced excitedly to her parents, 'I have a friend!' Her dad gently removed a desert scorpion from her face!

4 When it comes to birthday presents Bindi is one lucky girl! For her fifth birthday her dad gave her a cheetah – a live one!

5 This little wild child was destined to be a big influence in wildlife conservation from birth. She was even named after one of the animals. Bindi's name comes from one of the zoo's crocs and Sue, her middle name, is after her dad's beloved dog Sui. The name Bindi means 'young girl' in a local Aboriginal language.

12

Wild Word Search

Bindi loves puzzles and word games, especially if they involve animals.
See if you can find the hidden words in this find-a-word!

```
N O E L E M A H C D
T Y C I M E H O G T
N E A O I N Y N O A
A H F N M X E I R R
H A I F P M N H I B
P T R L A H A R L E
E E A R L R E L A Z
L E F G A I Z A A
E H A D I K C G O F
U C S M E E R K A T
```

CHAMELEON   SAFARI   HYENA

ZEBRA   CHEETAH   IMPALA

LION   ELEPHANT   MEERKAT

RHINO   GIRAFFE   GORILLA

Recipe·Recipe·Recipe

Sensational Sushi!

You will need:

1/3 cup mayonnaise
2 soft-boiled eggs
1/4 cup grated cheese
2 tblsp chopped chives
1 celery stick, finely diced
1 carrot, finely diced
1 tblsp hoisin sauce
1 tblsp honey
10 sheets nori seaweed
2 cups cooked sushi rice
2 tblsp sushi vinegar
soy sauce to serve

Steps:

1. Combine mayonnaise, eggs and cheese in a bowl. Mix together and add chives. Set aside.

2. Dice celery and carrots. In a separate bowl combine vegetables with hoisin sauce and honey. Set aside.

3. Place nori sheet on a sushi mat and spread with rice, leaving a 2 cm border at the top.

4. Spread with mayonnaise mix across the middle.

5. Top with vegetable mix.

6. Lift the edge of the mat, slowly rolling it away from you. Use gentle pressure and roll until ends form a join. Seal with water and vinegar.

7. Remove mat and slice.

8. Repeat with remaining ingredients and serve with soy sauce.

Wildlife Adventures Animal Profile

The GREEN-WINGED MACAW fact file

- Green-winged macaws are widespread in the forests and woodlands of northern and central South America. However, numbers have been declining in recent years due to habitat loss and illegal capture for the pet trade.

- In the wild their diet consists of fruits and nuts.

- Their large curved beak is used for cracking nuts and acts as an aid in climbing.

- Green-winged macaws grow to lengths of up to 90 centimetres and they have a wingspan of up to 1.2 metres.

- Macaws also have the 'zygodactyl' foot configuration with two middle toes facing forward and the two outside toes facing backward. This helps them to hold food and climb.

- Macaws create nests in holes near the tops of trees. Usually two eggs are laid by the female with an incubation period of 24–26 days.

- The young are fledged in 13 weeks and reach adulthood in six months.

For an exciting adventure story featuring the green-winged macaw, read a copy of

Bindi Wildlife Adventures
BOOK 1 – Trouble at the Zoo

The ULTIMATE
Bindi Q and A

Bindi answers the questions
you've always wanted to ask!

Who is your favourite eco-hero?

My heroes are my mum and my dad because they have taught me so much and they are my inspiration. I just hope I can be like them when I grow up.

Who is the most famous person you have met?

The Dalai Lama. He's not just a famous person but a great spiritual leader who is trying to make the world a better place.

What is your life ambition?

To teach people about wildlife and how to take care of our environment because every time we lose an animal species it's like losing a brick from the house, pretty soon the whole house will fall down.

What's your best moment to date?

The best moment of my life was when my brother was born. He is the light of my life. He is the best little brother in the world and I cherish every moment with him.

If you could be an animal what would you be?

I would love to be an eagle because I could fly high in the sky and watch over our world.

What's a funny fact about you?

Some of my friends were playing with dolls but when I was little I would sit in the enclosure with the newly hatched Burmese pythons and play for ages!

19

Bindi's Scrapbook

What an incredible, action-packed life Bindi has led!
Here is a very personal journey through some of her favourite
snapshot memories of family and friends – both human and animal!

I was just four years old when I got to join my mum and dad on their movie promotion tour. We would travel from city to city throughout the United States in the MGM company jet – sometimes I would fall asleep in the car, sleep through the plane ride, and wake up in a car in a completely different state! My favourite part of the trip was the time I got to spend with my mum and dad. It was during this trip that my dad taught me how to write my name.

When I was five years old I wanted to be just like my dad and ride a motorbike. My dad never rode on the highway, he just used his motorbike to get around Australia Zoo and our conservation properties. I was so thrilled and surprised when I woke up on my birthday to discover that Dad had bought me a brand-new Pee Wee 50. The bike was blue and white and I also got a helmet, gloves, elbow pads, knee pads and boots. It felt so amazing to sit on my very own motorbike. It took a lot of practice to master riding it. I would learn in a section of the zoo that used to be a turf farm. Flat ground, no obstacles and super safe. When Dad was sure that I had the hang of it we took our motorbikes out west to our conservation property near St George. Dad had built an airstrip on the property and we used it as our race track. I don't think I was actually going that fast, but I felt like I was flying.

Wildlife Adventures Animal Profile

The GIANT SABLE ANTELOPE fact file

- The giant sable antelope is a native species of Angola, in West Africa. It plays an important role in Angolan society, where it is the basis of many local legends.

- People thought it was extinct but then the species was rediscovered in 2002 at the end of the Angolan civil war, which had lasted for 27 years.

- It is a large, rare subspecies of sable antelope and is critically endangered. It is protected in national parks, and hunting it is illegal.

- Giant sable antelopes live in forests near water, where leaves and tree sprouts are always juicy and abundant.

- They are herbivores, and feed on foliage, medium length grass, leaves and herbs, particularly those that grow on termite mounds.

- For the first three years of life, male and female giant sable antelopes look almost identical. At that stage, the male develops a darker colouring and its curved, ringed horns grow to measure over 165 centimetres. Females' horns do not grow as large – around 142 centimetres.

- Giant sable antelopes live in herds of 10–30 individuals, usually females and their young, headed by one male.

For an exciting adventure story featuring the
giant sable antelope, read a copy of

Bindi Wildlife Adventures
BOOK 2 – Game Over!

Animals Are Our Friends

Bindi loves her best friend Rosie but she has lots of animal friends too! In fact, at home in Australia Zoo she's surrounded by hundreds of friends of the furry and four-legged kind! Here's what she says about her special connection with animals.

Why do you consider animals to be your friends?

When my dad first opened our Australia Zoo Wildlife Hospital he told me to always remember that each individual animal is important. I believe that when you appreciate every animal they become your friends.

From your observations, what sort of traits do you think animals show as friends?

An animal's greatest attribute, as with a human friend, is loyalty. An animal never judges, never argues with you, and never stops being your friend.

What are some of your favourite animals and why?

My favourite animal is the echidna because they are so unique in the animal world. They are monotremes, which means they are egg-laying mammals. And when the puggles hatch they don't have any spikes yet, so they are darling little fat pink jelly beans with long noses!

I also love snakes and crocodiles because my dad taught me that they aren't ugly monsters. For example, a male rattlesnake will protect his mate. And a mother crocodile is very tender and loving with her babies, carrying them gently in her strong jaws from the nest to the river when they hatch out.

Bindi's Top Ten Things You Can Do to Have Fun This Summer Holiday!

1. Round up some friends and go for an adventurous bushwalk or do some animal spotting. There are so many bird species to discover, so get a responsible adult to take you to some cool, but safe, places.

2. Go spotlighting and check out all of the cool insects and wildlife in your backyard at night time. Make sure you let an adult know what you're doing and have a torch with plenty of batteries!

3. Go to the beach with some friends and swim, snorkel, boogie board or surf in our beautiful oceans. But remember your hat and sunscreen!

4. Get your dancing shoes on and round up your friends for a boogie. You can make up some groovy moves and have a singalong to one of Bindi's *Kidfitness* CDs!

5. Practise your favourite animal noises with your friends. Pretend you're a cheeky tiger or a slithery snake. If you're feeling creative why not make a costume to match.

6. Come to Australia Zoo for the day and explore all it has to offer. From tigers to gorgeous elephants, there's plenty to see and do for the whole family.

7. Go through old magazines and cut out your favourite animal and plant pictures — you can create your own collage and frame it.

8. Get creative and make some animal cupcakes or yummy bickies.

9. Look into volunteering at your local animal refuge. You could help save a stray dog and find it a loving home.

10. Help save the environment and plant a tree in your backyard. Watch it grow and make sure it stays happy and healthy.

Save the Planet Bindi-style!

Bindi is well known for her passion for animals and the environment. She's determined to bring her message to the world – here are some of her tips for preserving our precious planet!

Why do you think saving our planet is so important?

Saving our planet is critical for our survival. If we cut down all the trees we will no longer have oxygen to breathe. If we kill all of the wildlife it will destroy the earth's system. If we poison the water we cannot drink. A great Indian chief once said, 'Only when the last tree has been cut down and the last river has been poisoned and the last fish has been caught will we realise that we cannot eat money.'

What choices do you make day-to-day to help the environment?

I believe even the smallest thing can make a difference. When cleaning my teeth I turn off the tap so I don't waste the water. Anything we can recycle we should. I open my blinds in the morning and use natural light rather than turning on a light in my room. I usually walk or ride my bike to school each morning.

When you think about the effects of climate change on animals, how does it make you feel?

Every time I think of what's happening to our animals and the environment I feel like crying, but I am determined to carry on in my dad's footsteps – getting wildlife into people's hearts. When you love an animal you want to save it. That's what we need to do to save all animals, their habitat, the planet and us.

If you could send one environmental message to the kids of the world, what would it be?

My one greatest message would be not to buy wildlife products. Many wildlife species are being killed for boots, bags and belts and for food and medicine. When the buying stops, the killing can too.

How can other kids try to be eco-friendly at home or at school?

Here's a list of great things you can do to help the environment:

- Turn off the tap while cleaning your teeth
- Recycle, renew and reuse
- Take the bus, walk or ride your bike to school or work
- Plant lots of native trees and flowers
- Pick up any rubbish you see so that it won't end up in our oceans
- Become a Wildlife Warrior
- Love all animals.

LOL!

Bindi believes in having a positive outlook on life! Stay happy and laugh out loud with some of Bindi's favourite jokes!

How can you grow a chicken tree?
Plant bird seed.

How does a camel hide from predators?
It uses camel-flage.

How do you stop a dinosaur from biting his nails?
Pull his foot out of his mouth.

How do you know when there are elephants in your fridge?
The door won't close.

How many giraffes can you fit in the refrigerator?
None, the elephants are in there.

How do you catch a runaway dog?
Hide behind a tree and make a noise like a bone!

What looks like half a tiger?
The other half!

Which day does a tiger eat?
Chewsday.

What do you call a koala that doesn't get out much?
A pouch potato.

What does a kangaroo say to its friends?
What's hoppin?

How does a pig write home?
With a pig pen!

What do you call a crate of ducks?
A box of quackers!

Where do calves go to have fun?
To the moovies.

What birds spend all of their time on their knees?
Birds of prey!

Which big cat should you never play cards with?
A cheetah!

Why did the emu go for a trip on the plane?
To learn how to fly.

What do you call a bunch of Barbies standing in a row?
A Barbie queue.

Wildlife Adventures Animal Profile

The KOALA fact file

- Koalas are not bears! They are actually marsupials that carry their young in a pouch.

- Koalas are found in eucalypt forests around the eastern and south-eastern coast of Australia.

- The koala's main food source, eucalypts, do not provide a lot of energy and for this reason koalas sleep up to 20 hours a day.

- 'Koala' comes from an Australian Aboriginal word meaning 'no drink', referring to koalas only occasionally having to drink water.

- Koalas have a great sense of hearing and an even better sense of smell. This is how they select which leaves are the best to eat.

- When a female koala is ready to breed she will call out to a male by letting out a loud snorting bellow. The female gives birth 35 days after mating.

- When born, the baby koala weighs only half a gram and is the size of a jelly bean (about 2 centimetres long). Its eyes open at 22 weeks and it grows teeth at 24 weeks.

For an exciting adventure story featuring Australia's cuddliest animal, the koala, read a copy of

Bindi Wildlife Adventures
BOOK 3 — Bushfire!

33

DIY
*Animal
Stories*

Here's a fun and creative activity for animal lovers! Bindi likes nothing more than hearing stories about animals and she likes to share her own stories by writing them down. You'll read one of her stories, *Candy's Day at Australia Zoo*, on page 100. Why not write one yourself?

YOU WILL NEED:
a pen and paper (or a computer), research books and your imagination!

Have a think about an animal you really like and admire. It might be a pet you know very well or an animal that lives in another country, which you may have only seen pictures of. It doesn't matter!

Find some books about your chosen animal and read up about it. You will also find loads of information on the Australia Zoo website: http://www.australiazoo.com.au

Picture your animal. Read as much as you can about your animal so that you can answer lots of questions about it. What does it look like? Where does it live? What does it eat? Where does it play? How does it interact with other animals? How does it interact with humans?

Once you feel as if you know your animal really well, grab a pen and paper. Get comfortable because now is the time to let your imagination run wild!

Start writing about your animal and allow a story to evolve. It's your story so you can let anything happen. You might be in the story or it might just be about your animal and its life. Either way, you will have written your own short story about an animal you think is really cool.

Make copies and show your printed story to your family and friends. You're now a published author and expert on an animal! Wow!

Crikey!
Crossword Puzzle

If you love animals as much as Bindi does, you'll blast your way through this animal crossword in no time!

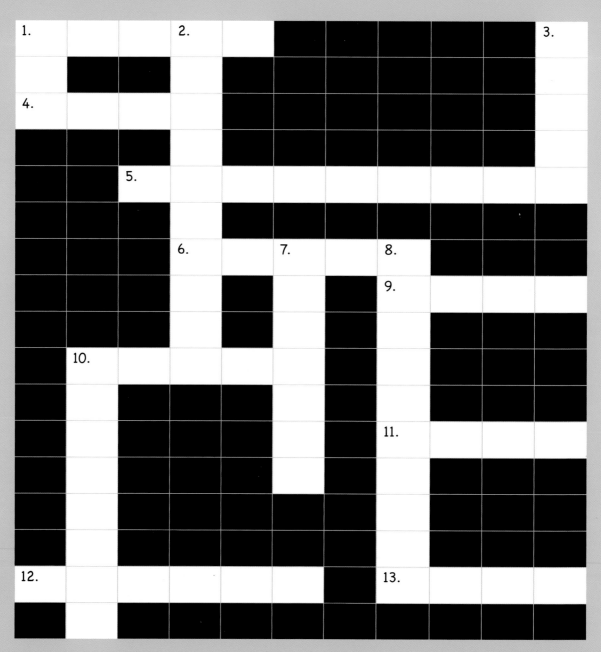

Questions

Across

1. The _____ Bear is the world's largest carnivore.

4. The Poison _____ Frog is thought to be one of the world's most venomous animals.

5. Excessive use of palm oil throughout the world is killing off which beautiful creature?

6. The Sumatran _____ is the smallest and most critically endangered of this Big Cat subspecies.

9. What's a camouflaged enclosure where humans can watch animals in their natural environment in the wild?

10. This Australian marsupial typically sleeps for 18-20 hours every day.

11. Found at the beach, these creatures walk sideways!

12. This Big Cat is very close to Bindi's mum's heart.

13. In Canada, slaughter of this beautiful animal is not illegal.

Down

1. What do you call a group of dolphins?

2. The ship *Steve Irwin* is protecting whales in the oceans surrounding which continent?

3. The smaller of the two types of elephant.

7. The tallest of all living land animals.

8. This large armour-plated mammal is prized for its horn.

10. A group of these Australian marsupials is called a mob.

Bindi's Scrapbook

My life changed when I was six years old because there was now another person living in our house. My brother Robert was such a special baby and I was so happy to have someone at home to play with. The only problem was that, as a tiny baby, he seemed to just take a lot of Mum's time and he didn't play much at all. I said to Mum, 'When is he ever going to be big enough to play with? Right now he's like a little loaf of bread!'

One of my favourite family filming trips happened when I was seven years old. We filmed a documentary for the Travel Channel and visited seven national parks in the US, from North Dakota to Texas. We travelled in a small motor home and since my cousin Brian did all the driving, my mum, dad, brother and I could play games on the long stretches of highway. We visited Mount Rushmore and Dad and I had the rare privilege of climbing to the top of George Washington's head. At the Rocky Mountains National Park we had lots of snow because we were travelling in November. It was the first time we got to build snowmen together as a family and we had some great snowball fights. We actually visited two national parks in Colorado and they couldn't have been more different – the Great Sand Dunes National Park had no snow and felt more like being at the beach. I got to meet a beautiful salamander and learn about local wildlife from Ranger Patrick. We ended our trip in Texas and I earned a total of seven junior ranger badges. There are nearly 400 national parks in the United States, so I have lots more junior ranger badges to earn!

41

Tips for Being True to Yourself

In her daily life Bindi juggles travel, performing, school work, sports, zoo responsibilities and finding time for seeing her friends and family! How does she do it? We asked Bindi how she strikes a balance in her busy life and finds time for fun and laughter.

What advice do you have for dealing with conflicts with friends?

Most of the time conflicts happen because of a lack of communication. Sleep on it and try to resolve the misunderstanding. Then talk it over in person to sort it out. Don't try to text your way to a solution.

How do you find the confidence to do what you do (performing, public speaking, etc.)?

I am very lucky to have had the love and support of my parents to encourage and teach me how to talk to a camera and speak in front of a group of people. Because I started learning at such a young age and watched my mum and dad, it has never seemed too scary. My dad taught me to speak to the camera as if it were another person. And Mum has always told me to just relax and be myself when addressing a group of people. I still get butterflies before I sing or dance on stage, but once I get out there I just feel at home. I think it's normal to get a few butterflies and I think I always will!

What are some of your fears and how do you overcome them?

I'm a bit sensitive about scary movies. If I accidentally watch something that might give me nightmares, I focus on all the happy things that I did during the day so then there's no room for bad thoughts.

How do you deal with life's frustrations?

Sometimes you have to deal with frustrating things, but if you concentrate on how to change things in the future, you can avoid putting up with a frustrating situation again.

How do you know when you're making a decision that's right for you?

Any decision has to be carefully weighed up. Identify the risks involved and all the pros and cons. After thinking with your mind, don't forget to trust your heart. Your first instincts are almost always right.

Do you ever worry about what others think of you?

It's a waste of time to just sit around and worry about what others think of you. As long as you're doing your best, you really don't have anything to worry about anyway.

What tips would you give others for being true to yourself?

Being true to yourself means standing up for what you believe in and not letting anyone push you to be someone you're not.

What are some of your favourite things to do to have fun?

I am very lucky to live in Australia in the middle of Australia Zoo. I get to do lots of fun things like surfing, horseback riding, playing with my best friend, hanging out with the animals at the zoo, and going on picnics with my brother.

Wildlife Adventures Animal Profile

The KOMODO DRAGON fact file

- The Komodo dragon is the largest lizard and can be found on the Indonesian Islands of Komodo, Rintja, Padar, Flores, Gili, Mota and Owadi Sami.

- They can grow to lengths of over 3 metres and weigh up to 100 kilograms.

- Their saliva contains poisonous bacteria which will disable prey. The bacteria will cause infection and wounded prey will often die within 2–3 days.

- They inhabit lowland areas, and mainly open grasslands, although hatchlings will usually inhabit more forested areas and are primarily arboreal.

- Komodo dragons eat almost any kind of meat. They will scavenge for carrion or stalk animals ranging in size from small rodents to large water buffalo.

- Baby Komodo dragons feed mostly on small lizards or insects. They do most of their hunting in the late morning.

- Young Komodo dragons are left to fend for themselves, living in trees for the first part of their lives.

For an exciting adventure story featuring the
Komodo dragon, read a copy of

Bindi Wildlife Adventures
BOOK 4 – Camouflage

WORD SCRAMBLE

Can you unscramble these words to reveal a special message from Bindi?

DLLFIWEI

ROARIRSW

EURL!

Tweets by Bindi!

I was so honoured to be nominated for an ARIA award. It was an amazing night!

Had a singing lesson and practised my song about saving whales.

Got to clean my cubby house today and it's sparkling!

Had a great surf!

I got to film with a Chinchilla! I named her Cotton. People really shouldn't buy fur coats!

Robert and I climbed a massive tree! I love spending time with my brother!

Thank you Edge for bidding on my Emmy nominations outfit. I don't know how you're going to fit into it, but thanks!

I'm so proud that Robert got named with me as Biggest Greenie. I think my little brother is a legend!

Got to have a great pizza night with Mum and Robert. My favourite pizza is Dominos Vegorama on puff pastry!

For school, I got to go to the library and pick out some awesome books!

Wow! What a great photo shoot yesterday! We had our pictures taken with lots of the animals from here at Australia Zoo.

Had a great Halloween, I got to dress up as a fairy!

The sleepover was so fun! I stayed up all night for the first time EVER!

Enjoyed the awesome roller coasters at Universal Studios. Went upside down like six times!

Had a beautiful salmon dinner with my yummy family... or is that the other way around? :)

Isn't it great running through the rain? I did it yesterday and it felt awesome!

I had an awesome time playing basketball with my own hoop this afternoon!

Top Ten Ways to Be a Zoo Keeper

Bindi wants as many people as possible to help animals. If you have a passion for wildlife and love animals, then being a zoo keeper could be your dream job.

Bindi shares some tips to help you achieve your goal!

1. Get fit. While it looks like cuddles from cute and fuzzies, zoo keeping is physical and hard work. It involves a lot of walking, physical exertion and working outside in all types of weather. A certain level of physical fitness is important for zoo keepers.

2. Take responsibility for your family pet. Make looking after Rover your responsibility and you will learn all about animals' needs, not just their food and water but shelter, exercise and entertainment.

3. Work hard at school. Many zoos require their keeping staff to have completed tertiary qualifications in zoology (the study of animals). To get this you need a degree from a university, which means you will need to do well in maths, science and English at school.

4. Learn. Today it isn't enough for keepers to look after animals. They also need to be messengers for conservation. It is important that they understand and can discuss issues threatening wildlife like habitat loss and climate change.

5. Get as much animal experience as you can. Not everyone can keep pets but you can volunteer your time at the local animal shelter, stable, kennel, cattery, vet surgery, zoo or aquarium. Some places might have age limits and long waiting lists so get cracking today!

6. Join a wildlife club. Your local area may have a bird watching club or a nature walking club. By observing animals in the wild you will have a better understanding of what they need in captivity.

7. Get involved with a conservation charity and sign up to receive newsletters from environmental organisations. This will help make you aware of current conservation and environmental issues.

8. Talk to people in the industry. Next time you are at a zoo or aquarium talk to the staff about their job and see if it sounds like something you would like to do.

9. Decide what is important to you in your life. Zoo keepers are committed to providing the best possible care for animals, and helping to make other people aware of conservation issues.

10. Animal documentaries are a great way to learn more about the natural world. There are also heaps of good animal and nature websites where you can learn more about wildlife.

Sleepover Secrets

Bindi's sleepovers at home must seem very cool to
anyone else – she gets to sleepover in a zoo every night!

The best sleepover Bindi-style involves:

* A best friend
* Some great music
* Delicious food like pizza
* Tip-top terrific games
* An awesome new flick

Bindi's best ever sleepover

My favourite sleepover was with my best friend Rosie.

We got to watch the movie *27 Dresses*, we danced to Jessica Mauboy
and The Veronicas and we stayed up all night!

We painted our nails, watched TV and best of all we got to see the
sun rise with a hot cup of Milo.

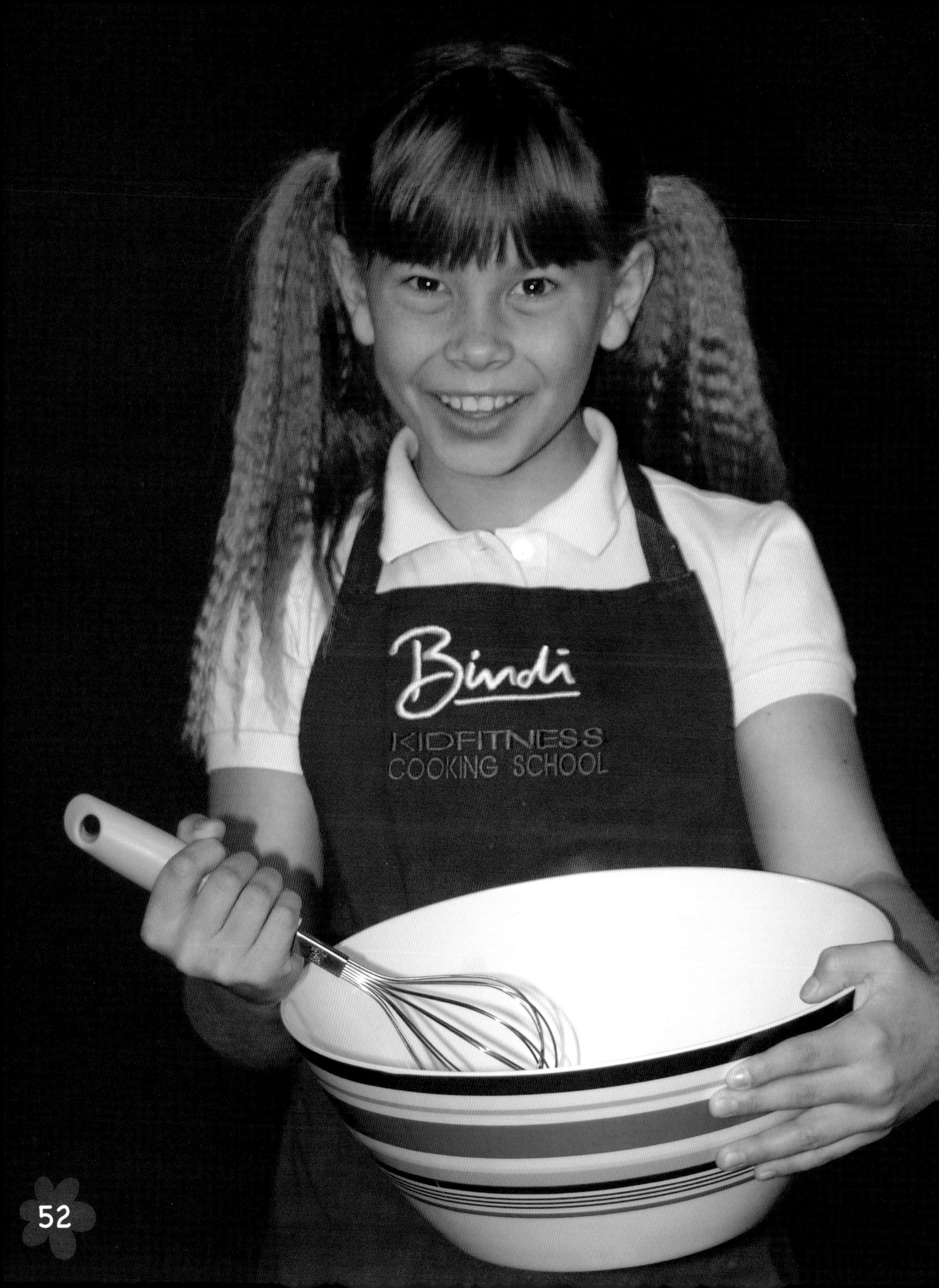
Bindi
KIDFITNESS
COOKING SCHOOL

Very Edgy Vedgy Wedgy

You will need:

1 large red or green capsicum
350 g cottage cheese
1 tblsp onion soup mix
1 bunch celery
2 carrots

Steps:

1. Cut the top off the capsicum. Carefully pull or spoon out the inside and discard.

2. In a bowl mix the cottage cheese and onion soup mix.

3. Spoon the cottage cheese mix into the capsicum shell and put into the fridge for approx 30 minutes.

4. Chop carrot and celery into bite-size pieces.

5. Pull capsicum out of the fridge, dip carrots and celery in and enjoy!

Bindi's Scrapbook

My last crocodile research project with my dad was at Lakefield National Park in Far North Queensland when I was eight years old. Dad was working with Professor Craig Franklin from the University of Queensland to track and study saltwater crocodiles. One day we caught a beautiful female croc in a floating trap. Dad got a rope around the crocodile's top jaw and carefully pulled her out of the cage. It was then that I found out dad was putting me in charge of the jump team. I would be the first in line to jump the croc's head with my dad expertly backing me up. I think my dad was way more nervous than I was! After pinning the croc down, we successfully attached the tracking device and measured her at about 9 feet in length. I named her Beauty and I have a photo of Mum, Dad, me and my brother with her. It was such a special day.

When I turned nine I had a Rock Star birthday at Australia Zoo. Not only did my favourite band, The Veronicas, play for 5000 people at our Crocoseum, but I got to go onstage with them to sing! Lisa and Jess gave me an autographed electric guitar for a birthday gift. I absolutely treasure it and I am so lucky to have The Veronicas as friends.

Fitness Is Fun!

Bindi's fave healthy snacks

- Fruit sticks are a very refreshing snack
- Cottage cheese on celery is not just yummy but healthy too
- Grapes in yoghurt is heaps of fun to make and eat
- Slice up a banana and put it in the freezer for three hours and you have a healthy treat!
- Pick out your favourite berries and put them in the blender, add some milk and you have a mixed berry smoothie.

Bindi is all about keeping fit and healthy and having fun all at the same time!

SURFING
Bindi loves getting up on the board and catching a beaut wave. It's cool to be able to surf just like her dad.

56

Bindi says – play your way to health and fitness

- Plan a treasure hunt to go on with your friends and family

- Climb a mountain, but bring your camera for when you get to the top!

- Pack a picnic and go to the local park or playground with your best friends

- Why not climb a tree, you'll feel like you're on top of the world

- Go to the beach and have heaps of fun playing in the waves.

JUMPING
Bindi loves jumping on her trampoline!
It's fun and it helps keep her fit!

Bindi's top five things to do in five minutes to keep fit

1. Play tag with your brother, sister and/or friend
2. Grab your skipping rope and jump with a friend or by yourself
3. Play some fun hopscotch and try not to fall over!
4. Dance to *Bindi Kidfitness* and not only will you be fit but you will be able to do some cool moves
5. Grab a ball and try dribbling. If you practise you can do some smooth moves.

MMA means Mixed Martial Arts. Bindi trains twice a week with trainers. It teaches her how to defend herself and it's a great exercise routine. She is now an orange belt and one day hopes to be a black belt.

Swimming

Twice a week Bindi goes swimming. She loves swimming and enjoys the feeling of being deep under water. Her favourite stroke is butterfly. Bindi thinks swimming is swim-tastic!

59

Best Buddy!

How Do You Rate?

You think you're a fabulous best friend. Are you really?
Put your loyalty to your best friend to the test with this fun quiz. How far are you prepared to go for your friends? Are you really as good a friend as you think you are? Find out right now!

1. What would you do for your best friend's birthday?
a. Buy her something you know she's wanted for ages and tell her what a great friend she is.
b. Throw an all-out themed birthday bash complete with entertainment!
c. Call her up and wish her happy birthday.
d. You don't know what date her birthday is.

2. It's a really hot day. You'd like to go to the beach but your best friend wants to go shopping.
a. Shopping's always more fun after a cool swim.
b. Go shopping. You can go to the beach anytime.
c. Flip a coin.
d. Go to the beach. She always gets her way.

3. **Your best friend calls in the middle of your favourite TV show. She's really upset. Do you:**
a. Listen to her, of course!
b. Turn off the TV and go over to her house to see if she's okay.
c. Put the TV on mute but keep watching as you talk to her.
d. Tell her she owes you big time.

4. **You argue with your best friend over something silly. Who apologises first?**
a. You both do. That's what best friends do!
b. You do. You're camped outside her house until you've both made up.
c. It depends on who was in the wrong.
d. You apologise first but end up making her feel so bad she apologises too.

5. Your best friend has a new haircut and it looks terrible. What do you do?
a. Turn up at her house with scissors, hair dye and straightening tongs.
b. Go and get exactly the same hairstyle to help her feel better.
c. Wait and see how she feels about it. If she likes it, then tell her you like it.
d. Tell her it looks terrible. It's better to be honest, isn't it?

6. Your best friend starts copying your dress style.
a. You're flattered. She must have good taste.
b. Awesome! You always wanted a twin sister.
c. Decide to always shop together so you can buy two of everything.
d. Ignore it. She'll grow out of it.

7. You both like the same handbag. What do you do?
a. You both buy the same one. Who cares if you match?
b. Tell your friend she should buy it.
c. Make a pact that neither of you will buy it.
d. You buy it first. You've wanted it for ages.

8. You're going to the movies. You want to see a girly film while your friend wants to see a horror film.
a. Explain to her you don't like horror films and hope she understands.
b. There are horror films with girls in them.
c. Decide to go for a bike ride instead.
d. Line up for a movie marathon.

How did you score?

Mostly As
If you're telling the truth then your friends are lucky to have you as a friend. You're incredibly thoughtful and caring, loyal and compassionate. You might be sainted. Friends may become irritated at your perfect ways.

Mostly Bs
Be wary of losing yourself in your friendships. People might take advantage of you. You tend to give too much away, perhaps to the detriment of your own identity.

Mostly Cs
You're far from perfect but you try your best. You sometimes get it wrong but your heart's in the right place. You're the genuine article.

Mostly Ds
It's time to go back to friend school and re-train! You could do with a gentle reminder about thinking about others' needs before your own.

You Can Dance If You Want To

Bindi has been performing to the public from a very young age! Singing and dancing are two of her greatest passions! She loves that she gets to sing about animals, how we can learn more about them and help protect them. Bindi performs regularly at the Crocoseum at Australia Zoo, first with the Crocmen, and now with the Jungle Girls!

Bindi has released two *Kidfitness* DVDs. The DVD-CD *Bindi Kidfitness 2 – Jungle Dance Party* is the follow up to the 2007 *Bindi Kidfitness with Steve Irwin and The Crocmen*. Both albums were accredited platinum status. In her DVDs Bindi gets to suggest lots of healthy exercises and teach kids some great facts about her favourite wild animals, all packed with a powerful, healthy punch.

BE KIDFIT!

On dancing with the Crocmen
The Crocmen are my dad's Wildlife Warriors and they sing and dance with me. It's stacks of fun performing. Sometimes I even get out of school early to rehearse!

On making *Jungle Dance Party*
The food fights when we were cooking were so much fun and the new songs are the best yet. I especially love 'The Four Macaws' – I think that's my favourite dance number.

On performing

I love doing this. Sometimes people who don't know me say, 'Oh, she's working too hard', but I'm not. I'm just a normal kid. I want to do this.

On stage fright

When I do my shows in the Crocoseum I feel really good. I feel like I can shine. I love seeing everyone getting into it, even the mums and dads. Before I do the show, I get lots of butterflies, but as soon as I run out the butterflies fly away. I always say the day you aren't nervous is the day you should quit.

On performing in the Crocoseum in front of 5000 fans

It is always so much fun performing on stage in the Crocoseum and being able to watch everybody joining in and having a good time. I also watch out for the best dancer so that I can give them a prize.

On feeling like a rock star

Every time I get out on stage I do feel like a rock star. What girl wouldn't? I love it because I'm singing about making a difference and making the world a better place.

On spreading the message

What I'm trying to get across is that the earth is in a lot of trouble. Our oceans are polluted, our trees are being cut down and our animals are being brought to the brink of extinction. I want people to know they can make a difference and help Mother Earth.

Wildlife Adventures Animal Profile

The WHALE fact file

- The blue whale is the world's largest animal.

- *Cetacean* is the scientific name that refers to whales, dolphins and porpoises.

- Like other mammals, whales breathe using their lungs. This means coming to the surface to take in fresh air. Most whales can stay underwater for half an hour before needing to take a breath.

- Humpback whales are known as baleen whales, as they have no teeth. Baleen are stiff, hairy sheets that hang in rows from their top jaws.

- Toothed whales and dolphins (e.g. orcas and bottle-nose dolphins) use echolocation for hunting and navigating, while baleen whales (e.g. humpbacks and blue whales) generally produce a series of sounds that are frequently termed 'songs' and are used for communicating.

- Whale songs consist of distinct sequences of groans, moans, roars, sighs and high-pitched squeals that may last up to 10 minutes or longer.

- Australian waters are home to 45 species of whales, dolphins and porpoises. Some of these species are permanent residents in Australian waters, while others are visitors, migrating from their summer feeding grounds in the Antarctic to the warmer waters of the Australian coast during the winter.

- The humpback whales that travel up the east coast of Australia from Antarctica do so for reproductive purposes. In the warmer waters they mate, give birth, and stay with their young, feeding them mother's milk until the calf has developed enough blubber to survive in the icy waters of the Antarctic.

- The round trip between Antarctica to the warmer waters of the Queensland coast is approximately 20,000 kilometres.

- Humpback whales eat krill, which are shrimp-like crustaceans. They sometimes go without food for six months while travelling north and time their return to the Antarctic in time for the krill spawn.

For an exciting adventure story featuring humpback whales, read a copy of

Bindi Wildlife Adventures
BOOK 5 — A Whale of a Time

Animal Antics

It's no secret that Bindi loves animals. She also loves to know quirky facts about animals. The more the merrier!

Did you know?

Wombats can look clumsy and slow with their awkward walk but they can reach speeds of up to 40 kilometres per hour for short distances!

Dogs say 'I'm happy' by wagging their tails.

Cats say 'I'm cranky' by putting their ears back.

Kangaroos say 'Danger' by thumping their hind legs.

Gorillas say 'I'm angry' by poking out their tongues.

Elephants say 'I love you' by entwining their trunks.

Chimpanzees say 'Hello' by touching hands.

Did you know?

Tigers are born with their distinctive black stripes. This pattern remains the same until they reach adulthood. These stripes are as unique to each individual tiger as our fingerprints are to us! Even if you shaved a tiger you would still see its stripes because they are on the skin, not just on its fur.

Did you know?

The **Tasmanian devil** can eat 40 per cent of its body weight in half an hour.

Did you know?

Tarsiers really can say their eyes are bigger than their bellies! In volume, the capacity of their eye sockets is larger than their brain case, and also larger than their stomach!

A **koala** will typically sleep 18–20 hours every single day!

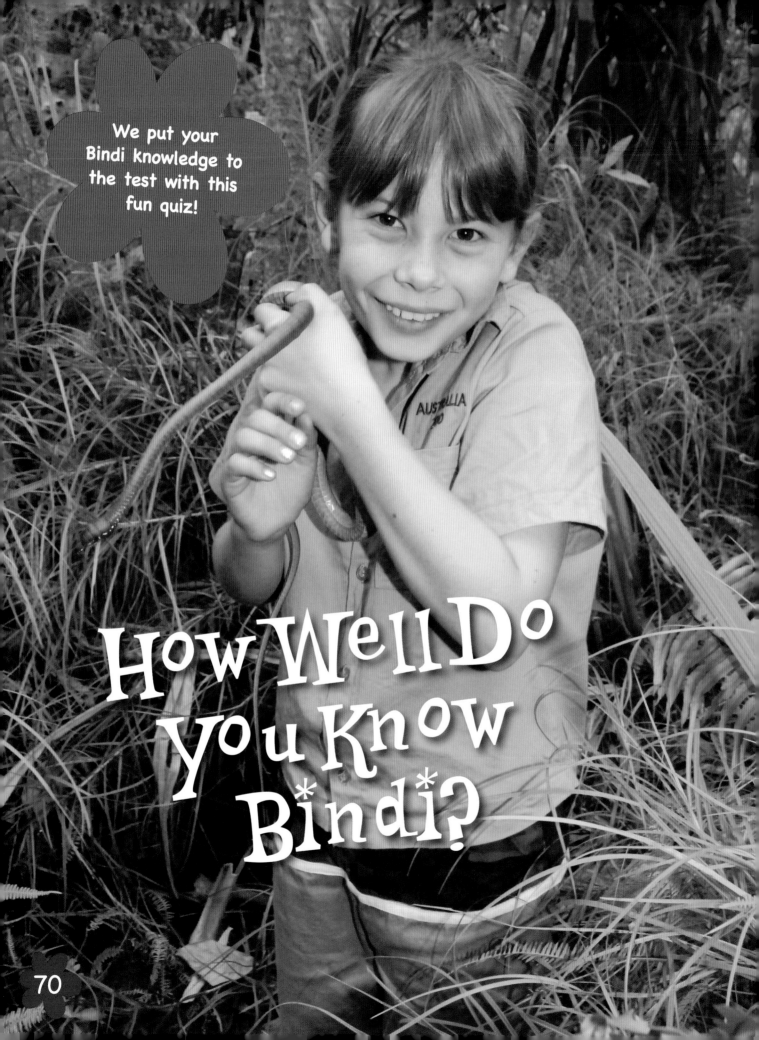

We put your Bindi knowledge to the test with this fun quiz!

How Well Do You Know *Bindi*?

1. What is Bindi's favourite animal?

2. How old was Bindi when she first rode a Pee Wee 50 motorbike?

3. Why does Bindi love animals?

4. What is the name of Bindi's first movie?

5. What was the name of Bindi's pet rat?

6. What is Bindi's favourite piece from Bindi Wear International?

7. Who did Bindi dedicate her 'Fave Aussie' award at the Nickelodeon Awards in 2007 to?

8. Which singer performed at Bindi's 11th birthday?

9. What did Bindi dress up as at Halloween at Australia Zoo in 2009?

10. Where was Bindi born?

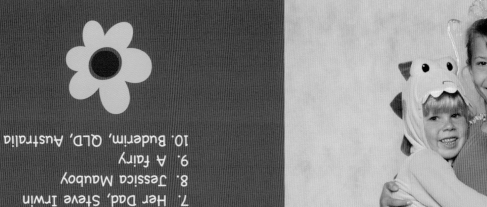

Answers:
1. Echidna
2. Bindi was five years old
3. Because they are so much like you and me!
4. Free Willy: Escape from Pirate's Cove
5. Candy
6. The pink jumper with her name on it.
7. Her Dad, Steve Irwin
8. Jessica Mauboy
9. A fairy
10. Buderim, QLD, Australia

72

Animal Cupcakes

Ingredients

150 g butter, softened
150 g superfine caster sugar
175 g self-raising flour
3 eggs
2 tblsp cocoa powder
1 tsp vanilla extract

For decoration
175 g icing sugar
2 tblsp lemon juice
A pack of colourful lollies

Method

Pre-heat the oven to 180 degrees Celsius.
Line a 12-cupcake pan with cupcake cases.
Crack the eggs into a cup and beat lightly with a fork.
Place all of the ingredients into a large bowl.
Beat with an electric mixer for two minutes until light and creamy.
Divide the mixture evenly between the cake cases.
Bake for 18–20 minutes until risen and firm to touch.
Allow to cool for a few minutes and transfer to a wire rack.
Make sure they cool completely before icing them.
To make the icing, mix the icing sugar and lemon juice in a bowl.
Ice your cupcakes.
Have fun with the lollies and create your own masterpiece!

True or False

Bindi knows lots about animals because she lives with them! Put your knowledge of animals to the test by answering True or False to the statements below. Answers at the bottom of the page!

1. The green sea turtle returns to the same place each year to lay her eggs.
2. Sugar gliders can glide through the air for up to 100 metres.
3. The dingo and wombat are on the Australian coat of arms.
4. The hippopotamus lives on land and in the water.
5. Dingoes bark at night.
6. Like most cats, tigers don't like the water.
7. Whales are not fish.
8. The jaguar is the fastest runner of any animal.
9. A giant panda is a kind of bear.
10. Apes are part of the monkey family.

Answers:
1. True
2. True
3. False. The emu and kangaroo are on the Australian coat of arms.
4. True
5. False. Dingoes don't bark, they howl.
6. False. Tigers are good swimmers.
7. True. Whales breathe air just like humans.
8. False. The cheetah is the fastest runner of any animal.
9. True
10. True

74

A Day in the Life*

Bindi has performed many times for a live audience and has even hosted her own television show – *Bindi: The Jungle Girl*. It's a children's nature documentary series. Bindi won Most Popular New Female Talent at the Logies (the youngest person ever to win the award) and a Daytime Emmy Award for Outstanding Performer in a Children's Series!

Hosting the show was lots of work and lots of fun! Bindi had to remember her lines, perform to the camera and handle animals all at the same time. You beauty!

1. My treehouse was lots of fun to film in because I had so many things to play with. I had a swing, ropes to climb, bunk beds, toys and plenty of animal friends. 2. I love filming with birds. Luckily, they like me too, because parrots in particular used to try to bite my dad!

# of a Jungle Girl!

Here are some of Bindi's favourite thoughts and memories from being a Jungle Girl.

Bindi: *The Jungle Girl is about wildlife all around the world and just how important it is for us to look after all animals. We have a stack of fun in my tree house but give a strong message about saving wildlife.*

The best part of filming this series was getting to work with my dad. He was so much fun and he taught me so much about wildlife and how important it is for people to care about animals. It was also fun working with my dad's best mate, Wes, and The Crocmen too.

3. The treehouse we filmed in was a bigger version of the original treehouse my dad built. 4. Some of the animals we filmed with, like this sea turtle, were rescued by our Australia Zoo wildlife hospital and would be returned to the wild. 5. It was fun to dress like an Indonesian princess with the help of our wardrobe wizard, April.

A Day in the Life of a Jungle Girl!

Dad and I had fun filming 'Bindo and Stevo's Cooking Showoh'. It was a cooking segment that sometimes got a bit wild. We even had a pie fight!

Wildlife Adventures Animal Profile

The SUMATRAN TIGER fact file

- The magnificent Sumatran tiger is found in the wild on the island of Sumatra in Indonesia.

- Tigers are the biggest of the Big Cats but Sumatran tigers are the smallest of the tiger subspecies; males weigh an average of 120 kilograms, while females average 90 kilograms.

- The pattern of stripes on their fur serves as camouflage, breaking up their silhouette so they are less visible to prey.

- Tigers stalk and pounce because they are not able to chase prey for a long distance.

- With over 80 per cent of Sumatra's forest already gone, the Sumatran tigers live within national parks. Their habitat ranges from lowlands to mountainous forests.

- The wild population of Sumatran tigers is estimated to be less than 500, making them critically endangered. Threats to the existing population are illegal poaching and loss of habitat.

- Kaitlyn, Bashii and Meneki are the names of the three tiger cubs that were the first to be exported out of Indonesia in 30 years. They were born on 4 December 2007 and first arrived in Australia in March 2008.

For an exciting adventure story featuring the endangered tigers, read a copy of

Bindi Wildlife Adventures
BOOK 6 — Roar!

Bindi's Scrapbook

When I was nine years old I celebrated two huge milestones in my life. I was so excited to be nominated for an Emmy in the category Oustanding Performer in a Children's Series. This was for my show *Bindi: The Jungle Girl*. We travelled all the way to America and when they announced that I won, I thought I was going to cry with joy. I was so proud to be the youngest person to win an Emmy and I was so amazed that I beat Elmo from Sesame Street!

After filming my first movie in South Africa when I was ten, I found it even more of a challenge to promote the movie when I turned eleven. *Free Willy: Escape from Pirate's Cove* was the fourth movie in the Free Willy franchise and went straight to DVD. The movie promotion tour took us to seven cities in North America including Toronto, Washington DC, Orlando, Dallas, Minneapolis, Denver and LA. I was proud to talk about how my movie character, Kirra, and I are alike. Kirra was trying to save a baby orca and I'm trying to save the Steve Irwin Wildlife Reserve from being strip-mined. I hope everyone enjoys the movie as much as I enjoyed making it!

FREE WILLY
ESCAPE FROM PIRATE'S COVE

ALL-NEW MOVIE!
ON BLU-RAY™ COMBO PACK & DVD APRIL 20

Wildlife Adventures Animal Profile

The SALTWATER CROCODILE fact file

- The crocodilian family includes freshwater crocodiles, saltwater crocodiles, alligators, caimans and gharials.

- Freshwater crocodiles have longer and thinner snouts, with a straight jawline and all their teeth nearly equal in size, while saltwater crocodiles have a broad, powerful-looking snout, with an uneven jawline. Their teeth vary in size with some almost twice the size of others.

- The saltwater or estuarine crocodile is Australia's largest apex predator and the world's largest reptile.

- It is thought that crocodiles live from 70 to 100 years of age.

- The saltwater crocodile is usually found in deep, dark murky water. It may inhabit fresh or salt water but is most commonly found in the brackish estuary areas of northern Australia.

- Female saltwater crocs can grow up to 3 metres in length, while males can reach 6 metres in length and weigh over 1000 kilograms.

- Saltwater crocodiles take a wide variety of prey, although juveniles are restricted to insects, amphibians, crustaceans, small reptiles and fish. The larger the animal becomes, the larger its prey is. Although a large male crocodile could take on a food item as large as a water buffalo, the majority of their diet consists of crustaceans, fish, turtles, small mammals and birds.

- Breeding usually takes place during the wet season.

- Four to six weeks after mating, the female will lay 40-60 eggs in her nest. The nest may be up to 80 centimetres high and is made of vegetation scraped together with her hind legs. Unlike many reptiles, the mother continues to look after the eggs, and once hatched, she takes her hatchlings safely down to the water to keep an eye on them.

For an exciting adventure story featuring the
saltwater crocodile, read a copy of

Bindi Wildlife Adventures
BOOK 7 – Croc Capers

Join the Call

Bindi says NO to Wildlife Products!

Conservation is not just about what you DO to make a difference; what you DON'T do also makes a huge difference to the world.

The future of our world's forests, home to many endangered species, is affected by what you buy. Many products readily available to us are sourced from illegal logging – but we do have the choice not to buy. In a more direct way, body parts of endangered species are still found in some traditional Asian medicines or sold as souvenirs.

Here are some simple changes you can make to your habits that will help save tigers and other endangered species around the world.

- DON'T buy products containing wildlife. Watch out for souvenirs and traditional Asian medicines containing body parts of tigers and other endangered species.
  Good purchasing habits can save endangered species.

- DON'T buy furniture that is made from illegally logged hardwood such as teak or mahogany. Only buy wood products from sustainable or recycled sources.
  Good purchasing habits can save habitats.

- DON'T support companies that directly damage the environment or support activities that destroy habitat. Only deal with ethical companies that don't consume wildlife.
  Put our planet first and profits second.

- DON'T remain silent. Speak out against environment abuse and unethical practices. Remember, poverty and human suffering go hand in hand with environmental issues.
  Speak out. Give them a voice.

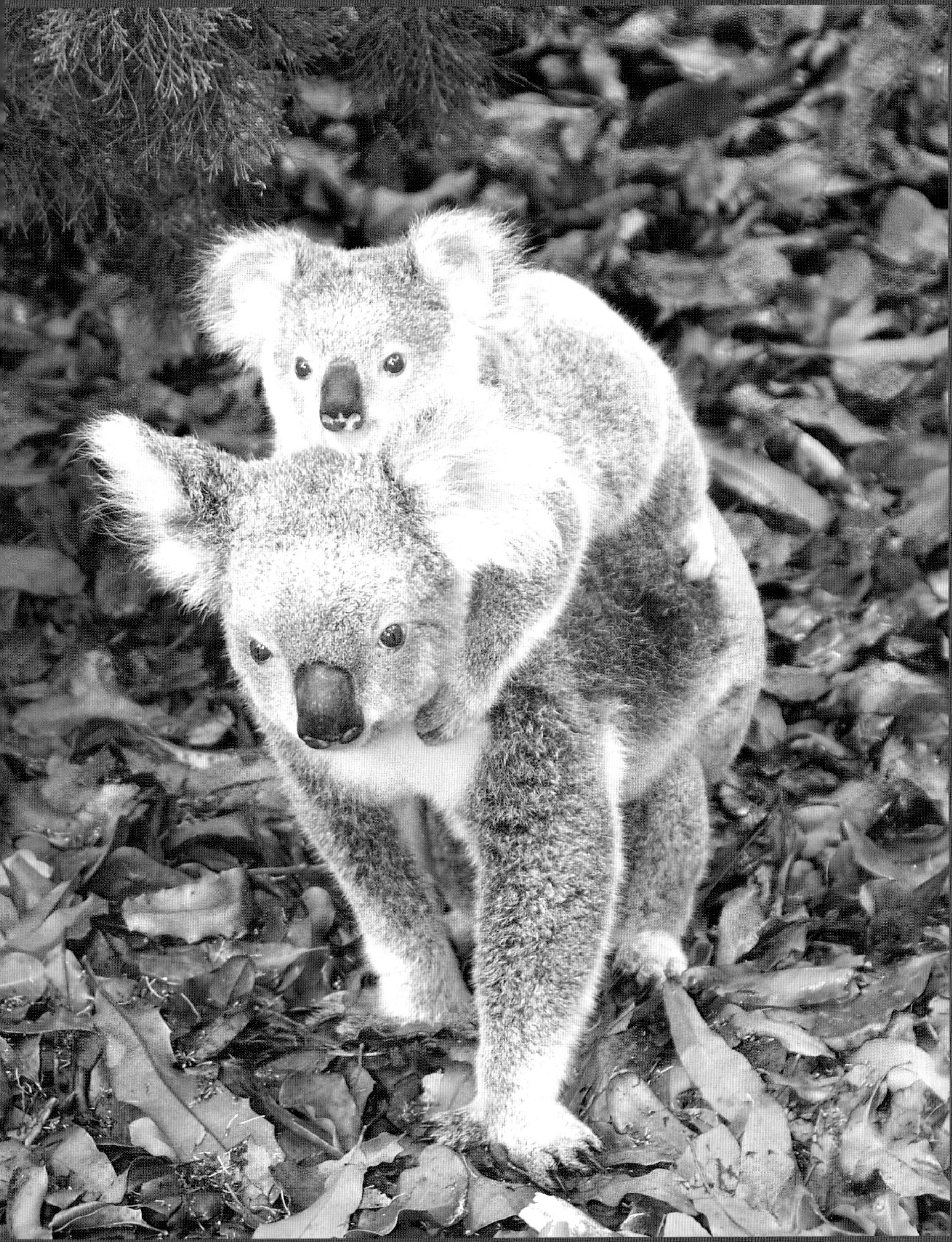

Join the Call Join the Call Join the Call

'Our love, passion, and devotion is to educate and share with the world our magnificent - often threatened or sometimes threatening – wildlife. Our job in this world is to bring misunderstood and feared animals (as well as the cute and cuddlies) right into your house, so that we can share and learn about the world's wildlife.'

– THE IRWIN FAMILY

Amazing Animals Quiz

Just how much do you know about the animals that live alongside us in our world? Take this cool quiz and find out!

1 Which animal is a reptile?
   a. Spider
   b. Crocodile
   c. Kookaburra
   d. Moth

2 Which is not a breed of cat?
   a. Siamese
   b. Burmese
   c. Arabian
   d. Bengal

3 What animal is the largest marsupial?
   a. Polar Bear
   b. Kangaroo
   c. Tiger
   d. Platypus

4 What is Australia's fastest animal?
   a. Koala
   b. Kangaroo
   c. Emu
   d. Wombat

5 A family group of lions is called a . . .
   a. Pride
   b. Club
   c. Lion Pack
   d. King

6 Which animal is a monotreme?
   a. Turtle
   b. Snake
   c. Echidna
   d. Horse

7 What do omnivorous animals eat?
   a. Meat
   b. Meat and plants
   c. Plants
   d. Fruit only

8 What do you call a baby hippopotamus?
   a. Junior
   b. Joey
   c. Calf
   d. Pup

9 What is a dingo?
   a. A slang term for lazy
   b. A type of sheep
   c. A scary creature
   d. A wild dog

10 The Great Barrier Reef is . . .
   a. The world's biggest swimming pool
   b. The world's largest coral reef
   c. The world's coolest place to snorkel
   d. The world's best place to find fish

Answers
1. B – Crocodile
2. C – Arabian is a breed of horse
3. B – Kangaroo
4. C – Emu
5. A – Pride
6. C – Echidna
7. B – Meat and plants
8. C – Calf
9. D – A wild dog
10. B – The world's largest coral reef

89

Best Ever *Birthdays!

Bindi sure knows how to throw a great birthday party! She's had her own themed parties at Australia Zoo since she was one!

Check them out:

Age 1 – Wildlife Extravaganza
Age 2 - Humphrey B. Bear
Age 3 - Opening new playground
Age 4 - The Wiggles
Age 5 - Pony party
Age 6 – Fairies
Age 7 – Shrek 2
Age 8 – Care Bears/Madagascar
Age 9 – Rock Star
Age 10 – Winter Wonderland
Age 11 – Masquerade
Age 12 - Bindi's movie premiere

Bravo

Bindi!

2 weeks old

✓ Bindi was born in 1998 and at only two weeks of age she took her first international plane flight to Texas. It was a trip of many firsts and here she had her first snake encounter!

2 years old

✓ Bindi makes her TV debut with her dad in *The Crocodile Hunter Diaries*.

4 years old

✓ Bindi makes an appearance in the Wiggles movie *The Wiggles: Wiggly Safari*.
✓ Bindi appears on *Oprah* with her mum and dad.

7 years old

✓ Bindi achieves a yellow belt in jujitsu.
✓ Bindi takes her 400th plane flight!

8 years old

✓ Bindi achieves an orange belt in jujitsu.
✓ Bindi participates in the 2006 MS Readathon, reading 25 books in one month and raising $658 for multiple sclerosis research.
✓ Bindi releases her first *Kidfitness* DVD.

9 years old

✓ Bindi hosts *My Daddy The Crocodile Hunter*.
✓ Bindi hosts her own show - *Bindi: The Jungle Girl*, debuting on Discovery Kids.
✓ Bindi appears on *The Late Show with David Letterman*, *Larry King Live* and *The Ellen DeGeneres Show*.
✓ Bindi launches her own clothing line called Bindi Wear International. One hundred per cent of the profits go to Australia Zoo's conservation programs.
✓ Bindi receives two awards at the Nickelodeon Australian Kids' Choice Awards – Fave Aussie and Biggest Greenie.
✓ Bindi participates in the 2007 MS Readathon, reading 23 books in one month and raising $2089 for multiple sclerosis research.
✓ Bindi is honoured with a Youth Conservation Hero award from the World Aquarium's Conservation for the Oceans Foundation.
✓ Bindi wins a Logie for Best New Female Talent.
✓ At the 35th Annual Daytime Emmy Awards Bindi wins Outstanding Performer in a Children's Series for her performance in *Bindi: The Jungle Girl*.

Bravo Bindi!

10 years old

✓ Bindi stars in *Free Willy: Escape from Pirate's Cove* playing Kirra, a young girl passionate about saving animals. Sound like anyone we know?

✓ Bindi launches her own Bindi Doll range.

11 years old

✓ Bindi is nominated again for an Emmy for *Bindi: The Jungle Girl*.

✓ Bindi is nominated for an ARIA Award for *Bindi Kidfitness 2: Jungle Dance Party*.

✓ Bindi and Robert receive the Biggest Greenie Award at the Nickelodeon Australian Kids' Choice Awards.

✓ Bindi is the MS Readathon Ambassador for 2010.

✓ Bindi launches her first series of adventure books – *Bindi Wildlife Adventures*.

Bravo Bindi!

WE CAN'T WAIT TO SEE WHAT YOU ARE UP TO NEXT!

97

Wildlife Adventures Animal Profile

The GREEN SEA TURTLE fact file

- Green sea turtles are reptiles, and are found throughout the world's oceans. Like the other six species of sea turtles, green sea turtle populations are considered either endangered or threatened.

- All species of turtles have evolved a bony outer shell which protects them from predators, as turtles are not known for their speed.

- When active, sea turtles swim to the surface every few minutes in order to breathe. When sleeping or resting, which usually occurs at night, adult sea turtles can remain underwater for more than two hours without breathing.

- Green sea turtles get their name from the colour of their body fat, which is green from the algae they eat.

- Adult green sea turtles are herbivores while juvenile green sea turtles are carnivorous. Their diet consists of jellyfish and other invertebrates.

- Although green sea turtles live most of their lives in the ocean, adult females must return to land in order to lay their eggs. This is done at night. Once the clutch of up to 100 eggs has been laid, the mother returns to the ocean and the young have to fend for themselves.

- The green sea turtle is one of the largest sea turtles in the world. It can weigh up to a massive 317 kilograms and its heart-shaped shell can measure more than 1.5 metres across.

For an exciting adventure story featuring
green sea turtles, read a copy of

Bindi Wildlife Adventures
BOOK 8 — Surfing with the Turtles

Candy's Day at Australia Zoo

by Bindi Irwin

Candy woke up in his little bed on Monday morning. He was thinking about what he would have for breakfast. Was he going to have a juicy carrot or a yummy piece of celery? When all of a sudden he remembered that this was the day he was going to Australia Zoo!

Candy hopped into his little red car and sped off to have an adventure with all his animal friends.

Candy arrived at Australia Zoo and handed over the money that he had been saving in his piggy bank. The nice lady handed him a zoo map and he rubbed his little paws together with joy!

Once Candy got inside, the first animal he wanted to see was the echidna. Candy was a bit scared at first to see such a spiky creature. Soon after he got to know him, Candy and the echidna became great friends.

Candy started to get very
hungry so he went over to have
a yummy carrot with the wombats.
They shared some really funny jokes
that made them all laugh.

Because Candy had a healthy carrot for lunch, he
went to get a tasty ice-cream. After the treat,
Candy couldn't wait to see more animals at the zoo.

Candy went to say hi to the little piglets at the kids' zoo. When he arrived, he saw that they had straight tails. Candy always thought that pigs had curly tails. They must not have curled them this morning, he told himself.

105

Candy was thrown into the deep end trying to wrangle Cameron the Crocodile. It took some strength, but Candy caught him.

Later, Candy signed up to volunteer at the zoo.
His first job was filling out some paperwork.
All the office girls were so glad to have Candy
as a new member of the team!

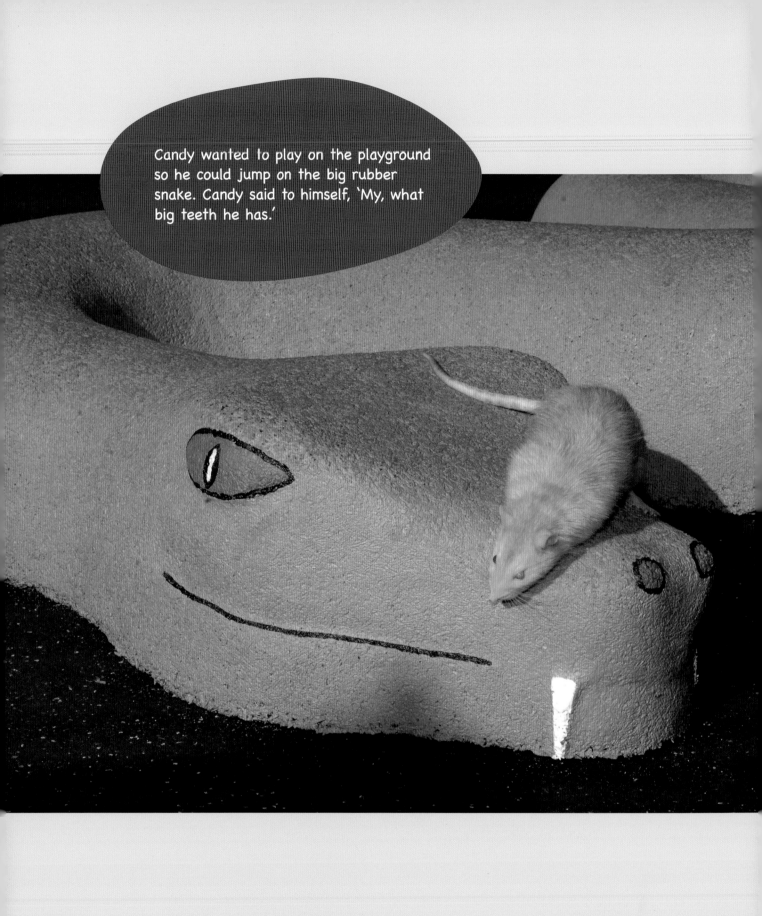

Candy wanted to play on the playground so he could jump on the big rubber snake. Candy said to himself, 'My, what big teeth he has.'

Candy couldn't believe that the gift shop sold rats just like him. It made him feel like the biggest superstar!

After a big day at Australia Zoo, Candy couldn't wait to get into bed and dream of all the great things he had done that day!

Candy was my best friend. I got him when he was just tiny. We did everything together! I took him around the whole zoo and we visited heaps of animals! So I thought I would write a story about the animals he got to meet. We had so much fun taking the pictures of Candy meeting them all. I hope you enjoy this story as much as I liked making it!

Thank you for coming on this adventure with me and Candy!

Love, Bindi